OBSERVER'S NOTEBOOK

BIRDS

PRINCETON ARCHITECTURAL PRESS • NEW YORK

$\frac{3}{4}$

BEE-EATER.

Merops apiaster, Linn.

Mintern Bros. imp.

Birds build nests in all shapes and sizes, and in all kinds of places, from small burrows underground to sprawling platform nests in the tops of trees. Birds use branches, sticks, twigs, and grass as well as mud, stones, and even spiderwebs to structure and insulate their homes. Some birds, such as orioles and weavers, make pendant nests that hang from trees (**1**). Some, such as woodpeckers, inhabit cavities in trees (**2**), while others build giant mounds of soil, sticks, and leaves—effectively giant compost heaps that give off heat as they decompose, warming the eggs. The most common and familiar nest is the cup nest. It is built by many passerines as well as hummingbirds and is often found on tree branches (**3**) or in tree forks, or even nestled on the ground (**4**).

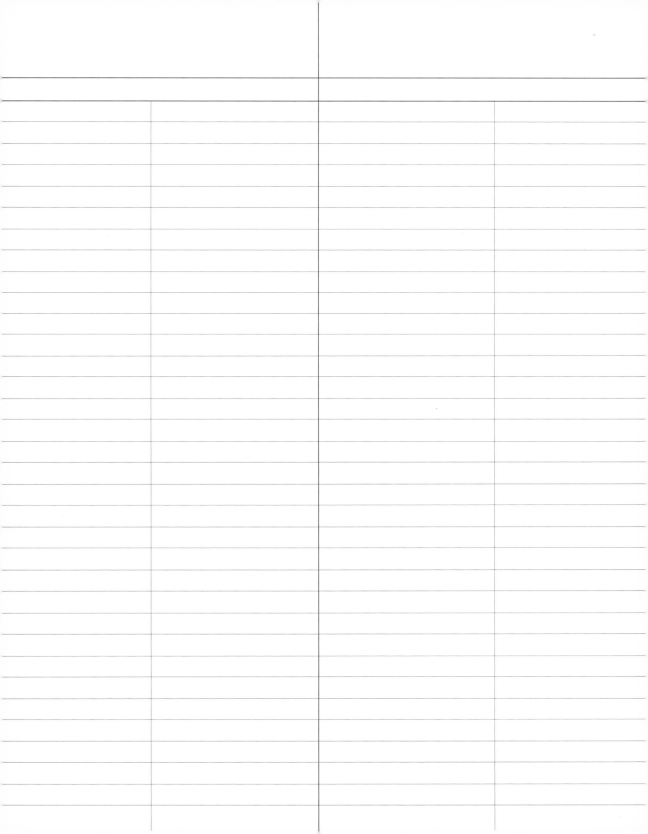

Imp. Becquet fr. Paris.

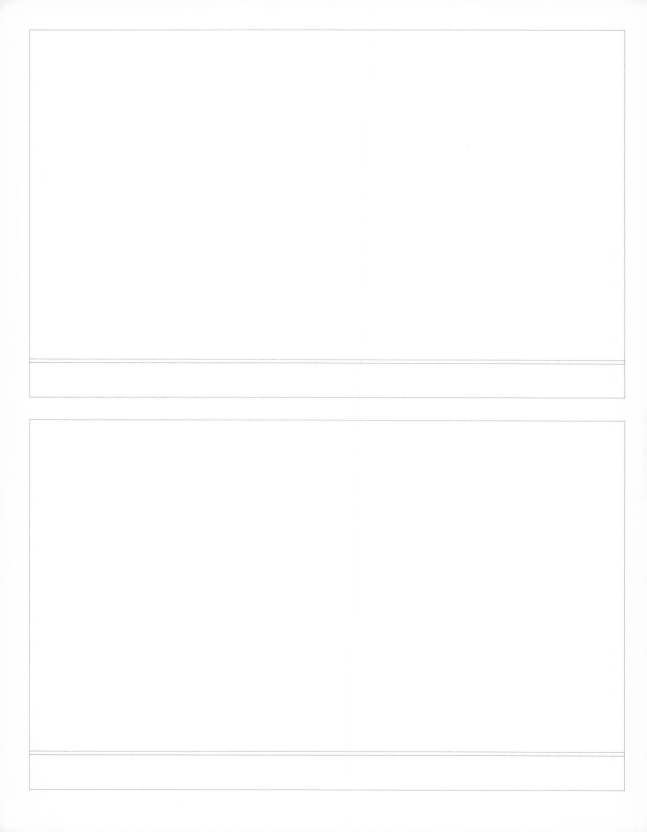

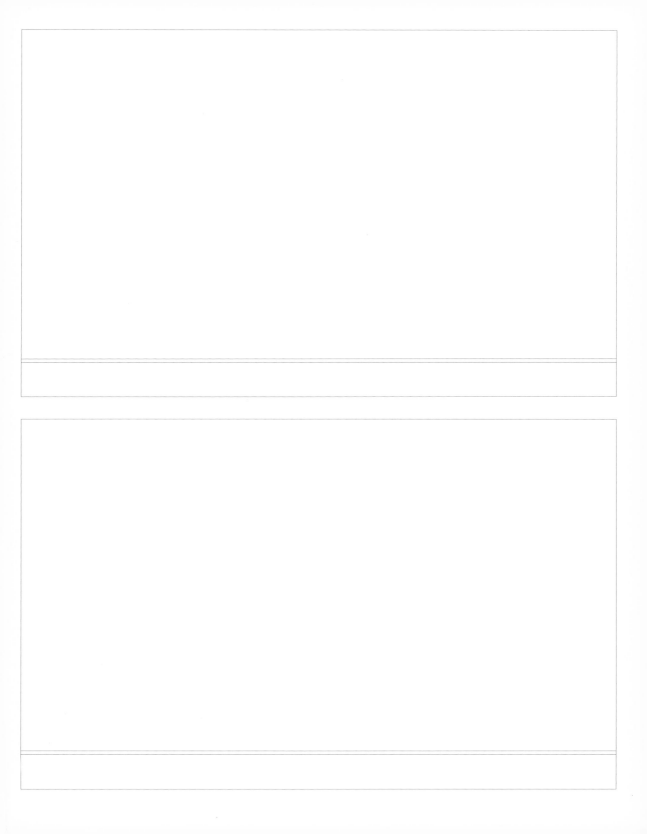

CRACKING
Cardinals, sparrows, finches

Short, stout, and conical beak
used for cracking nuts and seeds

INSECT CATCHING
Warblers, vireos

Slender, tweezer-like beak
for eating insects

DRILLING
Woodpeckers

Flat, pointed beak used for boring
holes into tree bark to find insects

SIPPING
Hummingbirds

Long, thin bill used to sip nectar

FRUIT EATING
Parrots, toucans, macaws

Large bill used to manipulate
fruit and break through its skin

CONIFEROUS SEED EATING
Red crossbills

The long tips of the beak's upper
and lower mandibles cross over
each other without meeting.
Used for dislodging seeds from cones

STRIKING
Herons

Long, broad beak pointed like a spear,
used for stabbing and grabbing

TEARING
Bald eagles, falcons, hawks

Strong, hooked beak used for
hunting and tearing meat

SCAVENGING
Vultures, buzzards

Large bill with a pronounced hook
to tear meat from carrion

SCOOPING
Pelicans

Large bill with stretchable
pouch for holding fish

STRAINING
Ducks, swans, flamingos

Broad and flat bill with comb-like
lamellae to strain small plants
and animals from water or mud

PROBING
Ibis, curlews, snipes

Long, slender, down-curved beak
for probing in mud for worms,
crustaceans, and insects

GRASPING

Owls, eagles

Clawlike, curved talons used
for catching and carrying prey,
characteristic of raptors

PERCHING

Robins, chickadees, orioles

Three toes pointing forward and
one back, for grasping branches;
characteristic of passerines,
or small songbirds

CLIMBING

Woodpeckers, nuthatches

Two toes pointing forward,
two back; allowing these birds
to climb up and down trees
looking for food

RUNNING

Emus, ostriches, cassowaries

Feet with two or three thick toes
all facing forward with flat base,
which enable flightless birds to
run at high speeds

SCRATCHING

Pheasants, chickens

Four toes, all with strong nails
for digging, characteristic
of birds that scratch in the dirt
to uncover seeds and insects

SWIMMING

Ducks, geese, swans, gulls

Webbed feet, located at the
rear of the body, which enable
propulsion through water but
make it harder to walk

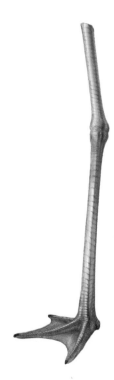

WADING

Cranes, herons, sandpipers

Long, thin legs and toes that
allow birds to walk through mud
without losing their balance

COLD & SNOW

Ptarmigans, snowy owls, ducks, gulls

Feathers covering legs and feet,
providing insulation and allowing
some birds to walk on top of snow

HAWAIIAN HONEYCREEPER

SILHOUETTES OF BIRDS IN FLIGHT

DUCK

THRUSH

KESTREL

SNIPE

SEAGULL

PIGEON

FANTAIL PIGEON

PHEASANT

OWL

American Sparrow Hawk, FALCO SPARVERIUS, Linn Male.1. Female.2. Butter-nut or White walnut Juglans cinerea

1. Cerulean Warbler.
2. Prairie Warbler.
3. Yellow Warbler.

4. Parula Warbler.
5. Blackburnian Warbler.
6. Black-Throated Green Warbler.

EGGS

**BARN
SWALLOW**

**CEDAR
WAXWING**

**HERMIT
THRUSH**

**WILSON'S
THRUSH**

**YELLOW-BILLED
CUCKOO**

BOBOLINK

**CARDINAL
REDBIRD**

**BROWN
THRUSH**

**ROSE-BREASTED
GROSBEAK**

**BLUE
JAY**

WHIPPOORWILL

**RUFFED
GROUSE**

**SPARROW
HAWK**

**SOLITARY
SANDPIPER**

KILLDEER

**SCREECH
OWL**

**RED-BREASTED
RAIL**

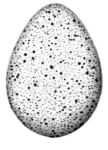

**AMERICAN
COOT**

**COMMON
CROW**

**AMERICAN
BITTERN**

WING CONSTRUCTION

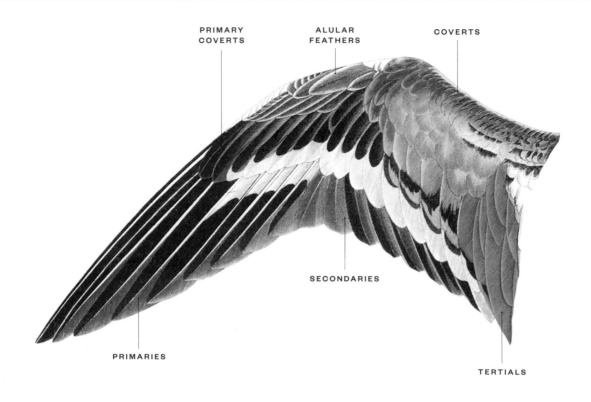

PRIMARY COVERTS

ALULAR FEATHERS

COVERTS

SECONDARIES

PRIMARIES

TERTIALS

WING ADAPTATIONS

GLIDING
Albatross, gannet, gull
Long, narrow,
pointed wings for long-
distance flying

SOARING
Eagle, hawk, stork, buteo
Shorter, faster wings
for riding thermals,
with feather "fingers" for
subtle movements

HIGH-SPEED
*Falcon, swallow,
sandpiper, tern*
Long, thin wings

ELLIPTICAL
*Sparrow, blackbird,
grouse, thrush, crow*
Short, fat wings, with
a lot of thrust and good
maneuvering. Not meant
for sustained flight

HOVERING
Hummingbird
Small, quick wings

COMPARATIVE SIZES OF BIRDS.

1. PENGUIN
2. TOUCAN
3. WHITE PELICAN
4. ROBIN
5. SNIPE
6. CROW

7. WILD GOOSE
8. SWALLOW
9. WILD DUCK
10. BOBOLINK
11. HERON
12. KINGFISHER

13. CORMORANT
14. AFRICAN OSTRICH
15. SWAN
16. BIRD OF PARADISE
17. FISH HAWK
18. EAGLE

19. OWL
20. STORK
21. CASSOWARY
22. QUAIL
23. PARROT
24. BALTIMORE ORIOLE

25. WOODPECKER
26. CONDOR
27. A BOY, 9 YEARS OLD

Scale of feet.

DOGWOOD

ELDERBERRY

HOBBLEBUSH

JUNIPER

PRICKLY PEAR CACTUS

SUMAC

SUNFLOWER

WHITE OAK

WINTERBERRY

Great Blue Heron. ARDEA HERODIAS. Male.

Watch and listen, take notes, make sketches, and keep lists of the birds you see. Notice the bird's size and shape, behaviors, and habitats. By making observations and asking questions, you can learn to recognize the birds all around you.

TAXONOMY

What family does the bird belong to? Does it look more like a duck, a sparrow, a hawk, a gull?

COMPARATIVE SIZE

Compare the bird to another of a known size—is it bigger or smaller than a robin?

SHAPE & STRUCTURE

Is it light and slender, or big and chunky? What about the length and shape of its bill, feet, tail? How many toes does it have?

BEHAVIOR

Does it walk or hop? Wade or swim? Hover, glide, or perch? Is the bird alone or with others?

FLIGHT PATTERN

Is it straight, undulating, lurching, soaring?

FIELD MARKS

Does the bird have streaks, spots, wing bars, stripes, a crest, or a mask? What are its primary and secondary colors?

SOUNDS

Is the bird's call a warble, a caw, a scold? Does it rustle or drum?

HABITAT

Where does this bird live? In the forest, prairie, wetland, desert, ocean?

SPECIES

DATE & LOCATION

BEHAVIOR & NOTES

SPECIES

DATE & LOCATION

BEHAVIOR & NOTES

SPECIES

DATE & LOCATION

BEHAVIOR & NOTES

SPECIES

DATE & LOCATION

BEHAVIOR & NOTES

SPECIES

DATE & LOCATION

BEHAVIOR & NOTES

SPECIES

DATE & LOCATION

BEHAVIOR & NOTES

SPECIES

DATE & LOCATION

BEHAVIOR & NOTES

SPECIES

DATE & LOCATION

BEHAVIOR & NOTES

SPECIES

DATE & LOCATION

BEHAVIOR & NOTES

SPECIES

DATE & LOCATION

BEHAVIOR & NOTES

SPECIES

DATE & LOCATION

BEHAVIOR & NOTES

SPECIES

DATE & LOCATION

BEHAVIOR & NOTES

SPECIES

DATE & LOCATION

BEHAVIOR & NOTES

OBSERVATIONS

SPECIES

DATE & LOCATION

BEHAVIOR & NOTES

SPECIES

DATE & LOCATION

BEHAVIOR & NOTES

Illustrations from "Nests" and "Eggs" republished in
America's Other Audubon, by Joy M. Kiser. Originally published
in *Illustrations of the Nests and Eggs of Birds of Ohio*, 1886.
Courtesy of the Smithsonian Institution Libraries, Washington, DC.

Special thanks to the Biodiversity Heritage Library.
www.biodiversitylibrary.org.

PRINCETON ARCHITECTURAL PRESS
A McEvoy Group company
202 Warren Street, Hudson, New York 12534
www.papress.com

Princeton Architectural Press is a leading publisher in architecture, design,
photography, landscape, and visual culture. We create fine books and stationery
of unsurpassed quality and production values. With more than one thousand
titles published, we find design everywhere and in the most unlikely places.

ISBN 978-1-61689-791-8
Manufactured in China

10 9 8 7 6 5 4 3 2 1

Editors: Sara McKay and Kristen Hewitt
Designer: Mia Johnson